Living in Christ

Prayer
Journal
2019-2020

This journal belongs to:

_____

© 2019 Novalis Publishing Inc.

Cover design and layout:
Jessica Llewellyn

Published in Canada by Novalis

Publishing Office
1 Eglinton Ave East, Suite 800
Toronto, Ontario, Canada
M4P 3A1

Head Office
4475 Frontenac Street
Montréal, Québec, Canada
H2H 2S2

www.novalis.ca

ISBN (for Canada):
978-2-89688-678-4

Published in the United States by Bayard,

One Montauk Avenue, Suite 200
New London, CT 06320
www.livingwithchrist.us

ISBN (for USA): 978-1-62785-452-8

Cataloguing in Publication is available from Library and Archives Canada.

Printed in Canada.

We acknowledge the support of the Government of Canada.

5   4   3   2   1   19   18   17   16   15

*God is closer to us than
water is to fish.*

—*St. Catherine of Siena*

Why journal?

SPIRITUAL JOURNALING IS a form of prayer. Far beyond recapping our life's events, the exercise of journaling helps us to express our spiritual life. Our written words capture our spiritual experiences, thoughts, struggles, victories – and essentially form a prayer through which we communicate to God what lies in our innermost self.

The exercise of spiritual journaling does not require us to be experienced in such a practice, nor are there any specific guidelines. When we journal, we need not worry about style or formalities. Just as in our regular prayers, Jesus wishes us to speak freely, simply and honestly what is in our heart.

This journal provides some guideline to your prayer exercise in the **Responding to the Word** section each day, where you will find a question that is directly connected to the readings of the day. If this question is helpful, feel free to use it, but do not feel constrained by it.

Spiritual journaling will essentially enlarge our vision and lead to a greater understanding of our spiritual journey.

Prayer for the Help of the Holy Spirit

Come, Holy Spirit, come
Let thy bright beams arise,
Dispel the darkness from our minds,
And open all our eyes.

Revive our drooping faith,
Our doubts and fears remove,
And kindle in our breasts the flame
Of everlasting Love.

Amen.

1st Sunday of Advent

"COME, LET US walk in the light of the Lord!" speaks a hopeful Isaiah to his weary, suffering people. We know this light today: it emanates from Christ himself, inviting us to venture forth from our inner dark places. Called to leave behind our anxieties, fears, discouragement and sinfulness, dare we emerge to be refreshed in hope and life with God and with one another?

Isaiah's message hits home in our world today, where unrelenting suffering and chaos are the daily lot of so many people. Deep down we know that we need God's help to finally renounce war and violence. We believe that true justice, peace and life-nourishing community are possible. Advent awakens in all of us the yearning to be more faithful to the liberating way of living with our God. As Paul says plainly, "Put on the Lord Jesus Christ."

What do I need in order to enjoy a fruitful Advent? A quiet, attentive heart, ready to listen to God's word within me; the willingness to be surprised by what I may hear or experience; a profound trust that allows God to light up my heart with burning love; and finally, a firm resolve to "keep awake" and not to miss the coming of the Lord. My vocation – our vocation – is to walk in Christ as a light to the world.

Rev. Michael Traher, SFM

People and Prayers to Remember this Week

Readings of the Day

Isaiah 2.1-5
Psalm 122

Romans 13.11-14
Matthew 24.37-44

Responding to the Word

Isaiah envisions a time of peace and fulfillment for the Jews. How can I encourage peace and harmony today with others?

Final Thoughts ...

Feasts this Week

December 3	**St Francis Xavier**
December 4	**St John Damascene**
December 6	**St Nicholas**
December 7	**St Ambrose**

2nd Sunday of Advent

IN TODAY'S READINGS we find a hope-filled theme that can be expressed in one word: change. Someone is coming; life will be different.

In the first reading, we hear of the unique qualities of the one who is coming and discover the wonderful changes that await us: former enemies will share food and rest peacefully with one another. This holy place will be filled with sacred presence, for only divine grace could make possible such change.

Commenting on his own unworthiness, John the Baptist recognizes this sacred presence in the One who is to come. John speaks clearly, certain of the need to prepare for the arrival of the Messiah. He invites listeners to repent, to change, to rid their lives of everything not bearing good fruit. Those willing to change – to prepare fully for the Lord's coming – enter the river, making visible their commitment to this new way of life.

It takes courage to change those aspects of our lives that are not bearing good fruit. Paul encourages us to rely on the scriptural promises of justice, righteousness and peace. We are wise to encourage one another in this new way of living. Today, on the second Sunday of this sacred time of waiting, we receive the invitation, the promise, and the food and drink that will sustain us. How truly blessed we are!

Brenda Merk Hildebrand

People and Prayers to Remember this Week

Readings of the Day —————————————————

Isaiah 11.1-10

Psalm 72

Romans 15.4-9

Matthew 3.1-12

Responding to the Word

The Spirit-filled Messiah will bring about greater justice and peace. How is the Holy Spirit drawing me to create better relationships in my life now?

Final Thoughts ...

Feasts this Week

December 9	**Immaculate Conception of the Blessed Virgin Mary**
December 11	**St Damasus I**
December 12	**Our Lady of Guadalupe**
December 13	**St Lucy**
December 14	**St John of the Cross**

Immaculate Conception of the Blessed Virgin Mary

MARY, MOTHER OF God, is often a larger-than-life figure for us, a woman set apart, honored for her "yes," her receptivity to divine mystery. But in today's Gospel we meet a surprised and confused young woman who is initially overwhelmed and reluctant to accept her call. This very human response is one that we, as fellow disciples, can understand; we know it from our own relationship with God.

Mary's story is so familiar that perhaps we don't relate it to our experience. We see the Nativity as historically grounded, over and done with, and so we wonder what her "yes" might say to us. Unlike Mary, we are not usually visited by angels with requests from God. We are not called, we think, to give birth.

Yet according to some mystics and theologians in our tradition, Mary's story continues among us. Her pregnancy, they suggest, symbolizes the process of discipleship: it mirrors our own service. With her we are called to bring new life into our world. Our passion for justice, our desire to alleviate suffering, to support the poor, the homeless and the abused, to teach, to heal, to create, to nurture are calls from God inviting receptivity, reflection and response.

Imitating Mary's courage, may we continue to give birth to Christ, to Love, in our time and place.

Ella Allen

People and Prayers to Remember this Week

Readings of the Day —————————————

Genesis 3.9-15, 20
Psalm 98

Ephesians 1.3-6, 11-12
Luke 1.26-38

Responding to the Word

Mary's "yes" profoundly changed her life and the course of human history. Where in my life am I called to say "yes" to God right now? What new life is God calling me to?

Final Thoughts …

3rd Sunday of Advent

ROBERT FROST'S POEM "Mending Wall" ponders the reality of barriers. History is full of barriers: the Great Wall of China; the Iron Curtain; the wall in Israel. I write this reflection from El Paso, Texas, where a metal wall separates its citizens from the neighboring city of Juarez, Mexico. We are really one community, split in two by a barrier that is both physical and psychological.

The Gospel addresses barriers in a subtle way. Behind prison walls, John the Baptist searches for the living Christ. Physically, he is walled in a confined place, but his heart is free. The Baptist is free because his questions make him so. No question can be chained. The prophet sends his disciples to Jesus with the question: "Are you the one?" Jesus' answer points to those who are free from the physical barriers of blindness, disease and death itself. Jesus, the Good News incarnate, is the source of all freedom.

Robert Frost writes: "Before I built a wall I'd ask to know / What I was walling in or walling out." During this time of Advent, let us become more conscious of the false barriers enclosing our minds and hearts and keeping us from being truly free. The Eucharist is a reminder that all are invited to the table, where there are no walls or borders.

Rev. Robert Dueweke, OSA

People and Prayers to Remember this Week

Readings of the Day

Isaiah 35.1-6a, 10
Psalm 146

James 5.7-10
Matthew 11.2-11

Responding to the Word

James counsels patience as we wait for God. What makes it hard for me to be patient this Advent?

_____

_____

_____

_____

_____

_____

_____

_____

_____

_____

_____

_____

_____

_____

_____

_____

Final Thoughts ...

_____

_____

_____

_____

Feasts this Week

December 21   **St Peter Canisius**

4th Sunday of Advent

THE FACT COULD no longer be denied: Mary was pregnant. Joseph, being "a righteous man," intended to "dismiss her quietly." He wouldn't make a big fuss. No need to make a difficult situation worse for the young woman. Joachim and Anne, Mary's parents, would have to accept her back. Obviously they would bear the shame along with her. There really would be little hope of escaping the gossip and judgment from their small, tight-knit community. As discreet as Joseph hoped to be, life would never be the same for them.

How many times has this happened to us? All the supposed facts are there in plain sight, just as they were for Joseph. We make our judgment, believing we are doing the right thing, and we prepare to live with the consequences. Only later do we find out that a larger truth had been concealed from our view. We just didn't see it.

Joseph had a dream. An angel of the Lord revealed the truth to him: the word of the prophet Isaiah was to be fulfilled. When Joseph awoke, he did not hesitate or doubt. He abandoned his previous resolve. Joseph took Mary as his wife.

As individuals or nations, let us pause in our rush to judge others. May we hear and see how Emmanuel, "God with us," offers grace and peace today to all.

Michael Dougherty

People and Prayers to Remember this Week

Readings of the Day

Isaiah 7.10-14

Romans 1.1-7

Psalm 24

Matthew 1.18-24

Responding to the Word

Jesus desires to dwell within us. What can I do to prepare myself for God's indwelling?

_____

_____

_____

_____

_____

_____

_____

_____

_____

_____

_____

_____

Final Thoughts ...

_____

_____

_____

_____

Feasts this Week

December 23	**St John of Kanty**
December 25	**Nativity of the Lord**
December 26	**St Stephen**
December 27	**St John**
December 28	**Holy Innocents**

Nativity of the Lord (Christmas)

OUR ADVENT PILGRIMAGE ends today at Christmas. How was your journey? Busy? Stressful? Peaceful? As you arrive here now, who and what is in your heart?

For me, a life-changing memory comes to mind – the wintertime birth of our son. We lived near the Arctic Circle where the winter darkness is long and harsh. The wilderness seemed endless. Yet, the wide-open sky, speckled with countless shining stars and bathed in the northern lights, awakened in me a sense of awe at the mystery of the universe. Inside the hospital, we waited expectantly, in our own Advent. Finally, at four in the morning, the miracle arrived: the first cry, the first embrace. A powerful mystery.

Of many special memories, none is more precious to me than the safe arrival of our son. It helps me to open a little window into the eternal mystery of Christmas. I imagine Mary and Joseph on a dark night, welcoming Jesus. I imagine a light shining in the universe – a light that no darkness could overcome. I imagine a radiant smile on the face of God.

Beyond the gift-wrapping, what will help us connect with the sacred mystery of this day? What dark corners in our hearts and bleak realities in our world still await the light of justice, goodness, mercy, compassion?

Steve Hill

People and Prayers to Remember this Week

Readings of the Day ——————————————

Mass during the Night:
Isaiah 9.2-4, 6-7 (Canada)
Isaiah 9.1-6 (USA)

Psalm 96
Titus 2.11-14
Luke 2.1-16

Responding to the Word

We must reject godless ways to enjoy the gift of Jesus. What must I give up in order to live more like Jesus wants?

Final Thoughts …

Holy Family of Jesus, Mary and Joseph

TODAY'S READINGS INVITE us to reflect on families other than our own. Above all, we celebrate the Holy Family as a model, both for biological families and for the spiritual family that is the community of faith. The Gospel focuses on Joseph's willingness to sacrifice his own desires and comfort for the sake of his newborn son. Mary is mentioned almost in passing here, but she too willingly accepted God's will for her in bearing the Son within her.

The other two readings also describe the ideal family. Sirach provides guidelines for how children should interact with their parents, especially as their parents age. This expands upon the fourth commandment ("Honor your father and mother"), which was addressed to adults, not children. In Colossians Paul starts by telling us how to relate to one another as members of the Christian community, then makes these principles concrete by applying them to the family itself.

The message running through these readings is the call to give greater attention to the needs of others than to our own desires. If we give our lives in service of others then we will be creating the family that God desires – in our families, our parish, our church, our community and, through them, in the entire world. An idealistic plan, yes, but the readings and the Lord who inspired them call us to nothing less.

John L. McLaughlin

People and Prayers to Remember this Week

Readings of the Day ————————————

Sirach 3.2-6, 12-14   Colossians 3.12-21
Psalm 128   Matthew 2.13-15, 19-23

Responding to the Word

Forgiveness is an important element in family life. Whom do I need to forgive and be forgiven by in my family?

Final Thoughts ...

Feasts this Week

December 31	**St Sylvester I**
January 1	**Mary, the Holy Mother of God**
January 2	**St Basil the Great and St Gregory Nazianzen**
January 3	**Most Holy Name of Jesus**
January 4	**St Elizabeth Ann Seton (USA)**

Mary, the Holy Mother of God

TODAY WE CELEBRATE Mary, woman of faith, woman of peace, whose radical "yes" transformed the world. Who is this woman we call "Mary, Mother of God?"

Mary held an open stance toward God, toward life, enabling her to face the challenges of her courageous "yes" to God. She was able to live with mystery. As a devout Jew, Mary listened to God's voice, discerning God's will for her. Her openness, love for God and courage to endure misunderstanding led this young woman to take a great risk and change the course of human history. Her strength came from the depth of her being. In today's Gospel, Luke says Mary "treasured all these words" and "pondered them in her heart." She lived the freedom of the spirit we all desire. This freedom came from the realization that God was with her through the pain and joy of her decision.

On this World Day of Peace, we have much to learn about peace from Mary. To bring peace to our world we must listen to God speaking to us in the events of the day, to voices from different cultures and religions, and to those with whom we disagree.

By reflecting on the word of God and the words of those around us we can deepen the peace within and, like Mary, help to fashion a more peaceful world.

Sr. Judy Morris, OP

People and Prayers to Remember this Week

_____

_____

_____

Readings of the Day ————————————————

Numbers 6.22-27   Galatians 4.4-7

Psalm 67   Luke 2.16-21

Responding to the Word

Everyone was amazed to learn about Jesus' birth. What has most amazed me about Jesus during this Christmas season?

_____

_____

_____

_____

_____

_____

_____

_____

_____

_____

Final Thoughts ...

Epiphany of the Lord

THE WISE MEN are a standard feature of our Christmas traditions. They appear in seasonal pageants and nativity scenes, greeting cards and decorations. Surprisingly perhaps, their only appearance in Scripture is this account in the Gospel of Matthew. Even here the details are sparse: no royal robes, no camels, indeed no mention of a threesome of travellers.

Based on this single scriptural reference, then, what do we actually know about these visitors? They are apparently learned and intelligent men, and – judging from the gifts they bring – also wealthy. What is clear is that their journey has been challenging. They set forth with no map and no clear directions, only their faith in the beckoning light of an unusual star.

At journey's end, they find a scene of poverty and simplicity. Far from being disappointed or discouraged, however, they are overjoyed. The uncertainties and problems of the journey are forgotten as they gaze in awe at the child before them.

Deep within ourselves, we too feel the pull of that star, the call to journey God-wards in faith. More often than not, the road ahead is unclear; we may be distracted by detours and difficulties or the deceitful voices of the Herods in our midst. Matthew's faithful seekers, travelling together in search of truth, are models for our own journey of faith.

Krystyna Higgins

People and Prayers to Remember this Week

Readings of the Day

Isaiah 60.1-6   Ephesians 3.2-3a, 5-6
Psalm 72   Matthew 2.1-12

Responding to the Word

Matthew's Magi remind us that we can learn about God from those outside of the Church. Who for me has been like the Magi, showing God at work in surprising ways?

Final Thoughts …

Feasts this Week

January 6	**St André Bessette (USA)**
January 7	**St André Bessette (Canada)**
	St Raymond of Penyafort (USA)
January 8	**St Raymond of Penyafort (Canada)**

Baptism of the Lord

THE INCARNATION DEMONSTRATES God's complete and total love for humankind. By becoming one of us, Jesus demonstrates the humility necessary to be of service to all of humanity. He is the embodiment of the Servant of whom Isaiah sings in the first reading, someone who sacrifices himself for the sake of others in order to be "a covenant to the people."

Jesus' baptism is just one example of this. When Jesus approaches John, John objects, because he is aware of his own subordinate status relative to Jesus. Moreover, John's baptism is for the forgiveness of sins, but since he is sinless, Jesus has no need of such a baptism. He submits, however, to provide an example of his willingness to give up his own position of importance, as well as to emphasize the means by which we are cleansed of sin. His submission is affirmed by the descent of the Holy Spirit, and by the message of the heavenly voice: "This is my Son, the Beloved, with whom I am well pleased."

Every time we participate in the Eucharist we celebrate Jesus' life, reminding ourselves of what he has done for us through his baptism, his earthly ministry, his death and his resurrection. We also receive spiritual nourishment through his body and blood, so that we are able to imitate him and be "a light to the nations."

John L. McLaughlin

People and Prayers to Remember this Week

_____

_____

_____

Readings of the Day ————————————

Isaiah 42.1-4, 6-7   Acts 10.34-38
Psalm 29   Matthew 3.13-17

Responding to the Word

At his baptism, God calls Jesus a "beloved Son." How can I thank God for making me a beloved child too?

_____

_____

_____

_____

_____

_____

_____

_____

_____

_____

Final Thoughts ...

Feasts this Week

January 13	**St Hilary**
January 17	**St Anthony**

2nd Sunday in Ordinary Time

"You have given me an open ear." This marvellous line in today's psalm evokes the basis for all discipleship, the possibility of vocation, "call." Just as the instrumentalists in a band or orchestra need an open ear so that they can tune together, so the Christian body needs an open ear so it can be attuned to God's call and presence and respond.

That openness is, of course, a challenge in our noisy, busy, distracting world. But if we are to create a "culture of vocations" – an ambiance in which believers can hear God's call – those open ears are absolutely necessary. But the ears may just be an image of the whole person – eyes, heart and mind – whose openness is needed.

God's voice speaks in the poor, and asks for justice and generosity in response to their needs. God's voice speaks in the lonely and marginalized, and invites our compassion. God's voice speaks in the cries of those oppressed by war, by violence and by injustice, and asks for our solidarity.

A culture of vocation cannot be limited to hearing a call to a state of life. For such a culture to thrive, our ears need lots of practice at hearing the divine voice wherever it calls. Whether our ears are seven years old or seventy, the better-tuned they are, the more fully we can respond.

Bernadette Gasslein

People and Prayers to Remember this Week

Readings of the Day ———————————————

Isaiah 49.3, 5-6   1 Corinthians 1.1-3
Psalm 40   John 1.29-34

Responding to the Word

Paul extends greetings of grace and peace to his community.
To whom might I extend a special greeting of peace today?

_____

_____

_____

_____

_____

_____

_____

_____

_____

Final Thoughts ...

_____

_____

_____

_____

Feasts this Week

January 20	**St Fabian**
	St Sebastian
January 21	**St Agnes**
January 22	**St Vincent (Canada)**
	Day of Prayer for the Legal Protection
	of Unborn Children (USA)
January 23	**St Vincent (USA)**
	St Marianne Cope (USA)
January 24	**St Francis de Sales**
January 25	**Conversion of St Paul**

3rd Sunday in Ordinary Time

SOMETIMES I WISH there were a step-by-step book for keeping my relationship with Jesus passionate and immediate. This book would instruct me on how to respond to Jesus' call the way the first disciples do in today's Gospel. When James and John leave their boat and their father to follow Jesus, they are to all appearances abandoning an aging parent and dooming the family business to disaster. It doesn't make sense. It's not even Christian! This is the way people who fall in love behave, disregarding everything the world sees as important.

But listen to that great lover and warrior, David: "Be strong," reads the psalm, "and let your heart take courage; wait for the Lord!" Don't listen to that cunning and strategic advisor, the mind; rather, trust our most intimate counsellor, the heart. Paul, too, the great intellectual, advises us today to mistrust "eloquent wisdom" and discover the "foolishness" of the cross. This heart-knowledge is simply unavailable to the mind.

"Repent, for the kingdom of heaven has come near," says Jesus. Here, at last, is an instruction for unlocking the knowledge of the heart. When we repent – when we put at the foot of that foolish cross all that weighs on our hearts – then we will be free of fear and find the courage and strength to answer Jesus when he calls. We will find the loving face of the Lord, right here already, waiting for us.

Louisa Blair

People and Prayers to Remember this Week

Readings of the Day

Isaiah 8.23 – 9.3 (USA)
Isaiah 9.1-4 (Canada)
Psalm 27

1 Corinthians 1.10-13, 17-18
Matthew 4.12-23

Responding to the Word

Jesus challenges us to repent – to change our lives. What changes might I need to make in order to follow Jesus today?

Final Thoughts ...

Feasts this Week

January 27	**St Angela Merici**
January 28	**St Thomas Aquinas**
January 31	**St John Bosco**

Presentation of the Lord

WHEN I WAS in high school, I learned how Shakespeare used the technique of foreshadowing in his plays. The chorus at the beginning of Romeo and Juliet, for example, or the witches' chant at the beginning of Macbeth, more than hinted at the coming drama in those plays.

In today's Gospel there is a sense of foreshadowing as well. Jesus was presented by his parents in the temple as part of the purification rite of the observant believers of his day. It seems a lovely tradition to designate as holy to the Lord a family's first-born. But the encounters with Simeon and the prophet Anna shocked both parents – and foreshadowed the young boy's future path.

These holy people were able to point to the fact that Jesus was the Messiah, and they also revealed just what that might mean. According to Simeon's canticle, Jesus was liable to upset the current order. He was "destined for the falling and rising of many." His teaching and witness would be "a sign that will be opposed." And those who love Jesus would suffer, as Simeon told Mary that "a sword will pierce your own soul too."

The challenge in our own faith lives is to accept to love and follow Jesus – even if our journey of faith might demand our purification, or even include sacrifice and suffering with him.

Joe Gunn

People and Prayers to Remember this Week

Readings of the Day ──────────────

Malachi 3.1-4
Psalm 24.

Hebrews 2.10-11, 13b-18
Luke 2.22-40

Responding to the Word

Simeon and Anna rejoiced when Jesus was revealed to them. Who has been a revealer of Jesus for me?

Final Thoughts …

Feasts this Week

February 3	**St Blaise**
	St Ansgar
February 5	**St Agatha**
February 6	**St Paul Miki & Companions**
February 8	**St Jerome Emiliani**
	St Josephine Bakhita

5th Sunday in Ordinary Time

IMAGINE A WORLD without salt, without light – dull, dark, insipid and lifeless. How often we take for granted these simple gifts of salt and light, symbols we ponder today as we reflect on the meaning of Christian discipleship.

For the people of Jesus' time salt was essential in a world without refrigeration. Its most delightful quality, though, is its ability to enhance the flavor of foods – not to give them a different taste, but to bring out the taste that is already there. A light is first and foremost something to be seen or it is of no use, just as salt without flavor is useless.

These images of salt and light are part of Jesus' Sermon on the Mount, spoken to those who lack material goods and wait for the spiritual blessings promised by God. It is a happiness that reaches its fulfillment through Christ. This is not law. It is gospel, good news. The law challenges us to rely on our best efforts. The gospel confronts us with God's gifts and invites us to claim them as the basis for our life.

By our baptism, we are the light that shines in the darkness. We are the salt that gives new life to the world.

Mary Ellen Green

People and Prayers to Remember this Week

Readings of the Day

Isaiah 58.6-10   1 Corinthians 2.1-5
Psalm 112   Matthew 5.13-16

Responding to the Word

God commands us to feed the hungry and satisfy the afflicted. In what ways am I meeting the needs of my community?

Final Thoughts …

Feasts this Week

February 10   St Scholastica
February 11   Our Lady of Lourdes
February 14   St Cyril and St Methodius

6th Sunday in Ordinary Time

IN THE FAST lane of life today, we are constantly challenged by a prevailing relativism – to make moral decisions on a case-by-case basis, and to put ourselves first, before considering others. As Christians, we must ask ourselves: how "relative" – if at all – is God's kingdom? Today's readings help us to answer this question.

Sirach says that "Before each person are life and death, good and evil and whichever one chooses, that shall be given." There are no gray zones here, no room for individual interpretation. There is but one right choice. The psalmist asserts, "Blessed are those whose way is blameless... who seek him with their whole heart." Our own idea of goodness pales beside the happiness and blessing that well up from the goodness of God.

In the Gospel, we hear Jesus demand that we seek God whole-heartedly. It is not enough to comply with an intricate menu of rules, hoping for some kind of automatic redemption. The gospel of love is uncompromising: anger is akin to murder, lust is as destructive as adultery and swearing falsely "comes from the evil one."

Let us give thanks for the gift of wisdom, which Paul says is "not a wisdom of this age or of the rulers of this age, who are doomed to perish," but God's wisdom born of love and spoken through his son, our redeemer.

Beverley Illauq

People and Prayers to Remember this Week

Readings of the Day

Sirach 15.15-20

Psalm 119

1 Corinthians 2.6-10

Matthew 5.17-37

Responding to the Word

Keeping God's commandments is a choice that we must make. What helps me to keep the commandments of God?

Final Thoughts ...

Feasts this Week

February 17   **Seven Holy Founders of the Servite Order**
February 21   **St Peter Damian**
February 22   **Chair of St Peter**

7th Sunday in Ordinary Time

THE SERMON ON the Mount expresses the very best of Jesus' message: the good news of a God who is a loving, caring, comforting and forgiving Father. Such great news entails great revelation too about who we are – children of God – and called to become "salt of the earth" and "light of the world." Knowing who God is for us and who we are to him can only be an illuminating and wonder-filled experience.

What Jesus tells us now is that we ought to rise up to attitudes and deeds that will mirror in day-to-day life our understanding of the God he is revealing to us. Jesus' teaching is first and foremost good news about the heavenly Father. Yet Jesus keeps inviting us to nothing less than imitating God. God is merciful? Be merciful to others. God is kind to all? Be likewise kind to all. God is love only? Be love only, even toward your enemies and those who persecute you.

So when Jesus says "Be perfect, therefore, as your heavenly Father is perfect," he sets the standard pretty high. Jesus himself has given us a shining example that living in the spirit of the Beatitudes not only gets us closer to God, but contributes also to make this world more humane. Isn't that a most thrilling and stimulating mission?

Jean-Pierre Prévost

People and Prayers to Remember this Week

Readings of the Day

Leviticus 19.1-2, 17-18
Psalm 103

1 Corinthians 3.16-23
Matthew 5.38-48

Responding to the Word

Jesus challenges us to pray for our enemies and persecutors.
How do I respond to those who hurt or offend me?

Final Thoughts …

Feasts this Week

February 26   Ash Wednesday

Ash Wednesday

As we begin Lent we hear Jesus speaking of what we know to be three Lenten practices: almsgiving, prayer and fasting. His words – which seem at first hearing to be a negative command: "Do not do these things in public" – are really an invitation to live in a way that expresses who we are as Christians.

Both the Gospel and the first reading make it clear that our almsgiving, prayer and fasting are not to be done to impress others – they are to reflect what it means to be a Christian. Since we live as members of a community, all three practices are ways of improving our relationships with others, with God and with ourselves.

Almsgiving is a way of sharing with others our gifts and resources, thus acknowledging the value of the other person. Prayer, which is dialogue with God, deepens our experience of God's presence, strengthens our knowledge of God, and makes us more aware of our dependence on the one who created us and sustains us. Fasting is one way to become more aware of who we are and what we place at the center of our lives.

The Gospel reminds us that Lent is a time to open ourselves to conversion, to a change of heart that brings greater life to us as individuals and to our community.

Sr. Barbara A. Bozak, CSJ

People and Prayers to Remember this Week

Readings of the Day —————————————

Joel 2.12-18   2 Corinthians 5.20 – 6.2
Psalm 51   Matthew 6.1-6, 16-18

Responding to the Word

Jesus warns against hypocritical behavior. What do I need to do to match my words with my actions?

Final Thoughts …

1st Sunday of Lent

WHEN I WAS a boy, this was one of my favorite Gospel stories. Three times the devil tried to trick Jesus, and three times he was easily defeated. At the time, I thought the story was about power – the power of good over evil.

But there are other important elements in the Gospel story, too. Its purpose is not just to give us an opportunity to applaud how much greater Jesus is than the devil, or for us to be spectators at a supernatural event. Jesus' temptation by the devil challenges us to be participants in our own spiritual struggle.

Our struggle is to see what is real – something that is not as simple as it sounds. The attractive illusions that the devil tempts Jesus with – bread made without work, the avoidance of death, the blinding brilliance of wealth and splendor – are very familiar to us. In fact, we're surrounded by them every day – in magazines, TV, movies, billboards, online. We are dazzled by them and seem all too eager to accept their glittering facade.

Jesus sees the temptations laid out before him for what they are. They offer emptiness rather than life. As the season of Lent begins, this Gospel is a call to us, too, to open our eyes and see the truth before us.

Patrick Gallagher

People and Prayers to Remember this Week

Readings of the Day

Genesis 2.7-9, 16-18, 25; 3.1-7   Romans 5.12-19
Psalm 51   Matthew 4.1-11

Responding to the Word

Jesus uses Scripture to give him confidence in temptation.
What can I do this Lent to make Scripture more important
in my daily life?

_____

_____

_____

_____

_____

_____

_____

_____

_____

_____

_____

_____

_____

_____

_____

Final Thoughts ...

_____

_____

_____

_____

Feasts this Week

March 3   St Katharine Drexel (USA)
March 4   St Casimir
March 7   St Perpetua and St Felicity

2nd Sunday of Lent

LENT CALLS EACH of us, inviting us deeper into the mystery of the incarnation. It is a season of active journeying with Jesus that forms us for discipleship. Transformation is the process of Lent; uncertainty and fear, its challenges.

Hints of Easter wonder are contained in today's story of transfiguration. Yet the resurrection is far off; the arduous journey to Jerusalem is still ahead. When we make this journey with Jesus each Lent, we are transformed into disciples. Although the dazzling light blazing from Jesus seems an appropriate image of God-come-into-time, for Jesus (and for us) living into "yes" occurs down the mountain, immersed in the holiness and wholeness of the everyday.

Abram, Paul, Peter, James and John are called from the known and the familiar to the unknown and the unfamiliar. Through their "yes," all are transformed by grace. Our growth into discipleship involves a similar spiritual movement from the known to the new, the unexpected, the illogical. Shaped through relationship with our mentor, we learn to see with Jesus' eyes, to discern needs, to respond freely in love to the many faces of pain and poverty we encounter.

Like the earlier disciples we can feel overwhelmed, fearful. We wonder how best to act in faith. To each of us today's readings say very simply: be not afraid. With Jesus, trust. Risk. Model your "yes" on his.

Ella Allen

People and Prayers to Remember this Week

Readings of the Day —————————————

Genesis 12.1-4
Psalm 33

2 Timothy 1.8b-10
Matthew 17.1-9

Responding to the Word

Paul reminds us that we are called to a holy life. How can I respond more generously to this call now?

Final Thoughts ...

Feasts this Week

March 9   St Frances of Rome

3rd Sunday of Lent

HAVE YOU EVER travelled to a place where water is scarce or unfit to drink? You will know what it is like to feel truly parched with no immediate hope that your thirst will be quenched. We can readily identify with the Israelite people in the reading from Exodus, who, having fled Egypt, now find themselves in the desert, desperately in need of life-giving water, knowing that they must move forward but fearful that they will die of thirst.

For Christians, Lent is that dry, parched, desert time in the liturgical year when we recall the 40 days Jesus spent in the desert in preparation for his ministry. In our parishes we experience this desert time when we refrain from pouring baptismal waters.

The prominence of water in this week's readings seems to drive home to us that we are still a long way away from the flowing waters of our Easter celebrations. We are only halfway through our Lenten journey. We must persevere.

Along with the catechumens and RCIA candidates, we take this opportunity to experience the unquenched thirst that comes with fasting and deep prayer. We pray that we might be purified, enlightened and truly prepared to bathe in the new waters of Easter. It is only then that we will be restored and brought to new life in water and the Spirit.

Connie Paré

People and Prayers to Remember this Week

Readings of the Day —————————————

Exodus 17.3-7   Romans 5.1-2, 5-8
Psalm 95   John 4.5-42

Responding to the Word

The Samaritan woman grows in her knowledge of Jesus through her conversation with him. How can I increase my time in prayer and conversation with Jesus this Lent?

Final Thoughts ...

Feasts this Week

March 17	**St Patrick**
March 18	**St Cyril of Jerusalem**
March 19	**St Joseph**

4th Sunday of Lent

"WE SEE WHAT we want to see," the saying goes. In other words, we usually think "inside the box."

Such is the case with the Jewish authorities in today's Gospel. They consistently attempt to discredit the miracle of the young man born blind rather than offer support, let alone celebrate his healing. This response is not only what is deemed appropriate, it is also what is thought to be real and true. Truth is found only within the realm of the expected – "inside the box."

Jesus, however, follows the love of his Father. Thus, during his mission among us, he consistently steps "outside the box," freeing us from the fear that restrains us all. Only love can cast out that fear, leading us to accept what is given, even though it might be unexpected or challenging.

The healing of the young man born blind is the sixth of seven key signs in John. As these signs accumulate, we are led deeper into an understanding of the Son of Man. Not only does Jesus become attractive beyond our expectations, he also calls us to a love beyond our imaginings. Love casts out fear, leading us out of blindness to see things we've never seen before.

What a wonderful metaphor for Lent, a journey which leads us further and further out of blindness into the light of resurrection.

Jerome Herauf

People and Prayers to Remember this Week

Readings of the Day

1 Samuel 16.1b, 6-7, 10-13
Psalm 23

Ephesians 5.8-14
John 9.1-41

Responding to the Word

The blind man learns to recognize Jesus through faith. What would most help me to "see" Jesus in a new way today?

Final Thoughts …

Feasts this Week

March 23   **St Turibius of Mogrovejo**
March 25   **Annunciation of the Lord**

5th Sunday of Lent

LIFE AND DEATH; hope and despair; the anguish of waiting – today's Gospel is awash with gut-wrenching emotion. Yet while reading the story of the death and resurrection of Lazarus, I sit content and self-satisfied. My heart remains indifferent and untouched. I know the ending to this drama and am expecting Easter.

Then I ponder. What is resurrection? What does it mean in my daily life? I remember a day last winter. Tethered to a trusted companion, belted securely into a "sit ski," I sat poised to take my first downhill ski run. As we took off, an explosion of joy filled my body. Handicapped since birth, I had never experienced such freedom... such wild abandon... such present-moment living! I squealed with child-like wonder as my hat took flight in the wind. A piece of my soul long ago buried was resurrected. That day I was unbound and set free.

When I think of my time on the hill, I realize that the experience of resurrection is a verb... a dynamic, vibrant, forever-in-motion verb. Daily Jesus yearns to reach down and unbind me from many death-like experiences. With Lazarus I can now hear the voice of Jesus calling me to full life. Willingly I stand straight and tall as Jesus unbinds me from that which hinders. Come! Experience resurrection as a verb!

Karen Johnson

People and Prayers to Remember this Week

_____

_____

_____

Readings of the Day ————————————————

Ezekiel 37.12-14   Romans 8.8-11
Psalm 130   John 11.1-45

Responding to the Word

God promises new life through the Holy Spirit. What new spiritual life have you felt this Lent?

_____

_____

_____

_____

_____

_____

_____

_____

_____

Final Thoughts ...

Feasts this Week

April 2 **St Francis of Paola**
April 4 **St Isidore (Canada)**

Passion (Palm) Sunday

THE LORD'S PASSION and death could lose its power in our liturgy because of its repetition. We can easily "drift off," for we know how the story will end. There are ways to keep the story alive for us, however. One way is to reflect on the Passion in the light of the other two readings.

Today's passage from Isaiah presents a faithful believer who, like Jesus, encountered opposition when he tried to bring God's word to his own community. Throughout history people have suffered and even died for their commitment to God. This happened long before Jesus and continues to this day. Some Christians still give their very lives as martyrs, literally as "witnesses" to the faith.

The second reading is an ancient hymn reflecting on the significance of Jesus' saving action for us. The crucifixion is the end of a process of "emptying" that began with Jesus' birth and continued through his entire life. His willingness to die for us is rooted in his willingness to become one of us for our salvation.

As we remember Jesus' sacrifice, let us reflect on the great love his death expresses, and how we are all called to empty ourselves as Jesus did, giving of ourselves for the sake of others. What does it really mean for me to take up the cross and follow Jesus?

John L. McLaughlin

People and Prayers to Remember this Week

Readings of the Day —————————————————

Matthew 21.1-11 (Procession)   Philippians 2.6-11
Isaiah 50.4-7   Matthew 26.14 – 27.66
Psalm 22

Responding to the Word

**God's servants endure much for God's sake. What suffering
has been most challenging for me to accept recently?**

Final Thoughts …

Holy Thursday

ASK ANYONE WITH memory problems – to not be able to remember is, at best, deeply frustrating. At worst, whole parts of one's life and identity simply cease to be. This day, this remembering of the Lord's Supper, is vital to our life, identity and mission as Christians. Today we remember one of the most intimate, moving and crucial moments of Jesus' life.

Our remembering is fourfold: Jesus shielding us from death, opening us to new life; foot-washing, which is the test of our discipleship and intimacy with Jesus; Eucharist, which makes real the saving death and resurrection of Jesus; love, which fulfills our life's purpose in bringing the reign of God to our world, in our lifetime.

Remembering must be grasped, solidified, made tangible, lest we forget and risk slipping into a kind of amnesia of the will and spirit.

Remembering isn't confined to church. Unless we remember in our lives every day – in our choices for justice and the poor, in our loving to the end of our energy and time, in our washing of the feet of the homeless and the hungry and the others around whom we are uncomfortable – unless our remembering is active every day, we are all talk and no action.

Remember with the community this night. Remember in your taking the bread and drinking the cup. Remember with your life... remember.

Sr. Phyllis Giroux, SC

People and Prayers to Remember this Week

Readings of the Day

Exodus 12.1-8, 11-14   1 Corinthians 11.23-26
Psalm 116   John 13.1-15

Responding to the Word

The sacrifice of the Passover lamb expresses the people's complete dedication to God and the desire to share life with God. What sacrifice must I make to rededicate myself to God today?

Final Thoughts ...

Good Friday

"FATHER, INTO YOUR hands I commend my Spirit." Surrender lies at the heart of today's Good Friday liturgy. Here we listen to John's Gospel, which makes clear that Jesus surrenders his life; it is not taken from him. Just as the Father so loved the world that he gave his Son, so Jesus loves us and, out of love, surrenders to his Father and to those who would kill him. In supreme trust and sure confidence, he empties himself of glory.

One of the most moving ritual gestures of the whole Church year is today's Adoration of the Holy Cross. It is an awesome thing to contemplate this symbol of Jesus' surrender, even as we watch those who approach it: the elderly, families with babes in arms, tentative teens, the grieving, the poor, the homeless, the rich, the outcasts and the pillars of the Church. The cross is the great leveller. Before it, all our trappings of power are revealed as empty; all our pretense is stripped. We have nothing to bring – or lose – but ourselves.

In this simple gesture, all surrender the burdens of the year, the losses, the pains, the fears, the defeats, the joys and the triumphs: their very selves. All come to the cross, its strong arms reaching out in tenderness, mercy and love to embrace and to save each one who approaches.

Bernadette Gasslein

People and Prayers to Remember Today

Readings of the Day ———————————————

Isaiah 52.13 – 53.12   Hebrews 4.14-16; 5.7-9
Psalm 31   John 18.1 – 19.42

Responding to the Word

John's Passion narrative traces Jesus' victory over sin and death. Which event in today's Gospel was most important to me?

Final Thoughts …

Easter Vigil

AS WE BEGIN tonight's Easter Vigil liturgy, our hearts are stirred by the lighting of the new fire and by having our candles lit to symbolize the risen Christ, Light of the world. The singing of the Exsultet lifts our spirits, and we cherish hearing again the stories of our origins and ancestors in faith.

Tonight's Gospel invites us to go with the two Marys, so anxious to visit the tomb where Jesus is buried. They did not expect to encounter an earthquake, the tomb stone rolled back, and angels appearing to say, "He is not here; for he has been raised." In fear and joy they run to tell the disciples, when suddenly they meet Jesus. Overwhelmed, they embrace his feet and worship him, their hearts telling them something wondrously new is happening.

Easter is not about passively contemplating an empty tomb. It's an invitation to encounter the risen Christ, to rejoice and to share the Good News. By his resurrection, Jesus reaches out to all who are entombed in the world, setting every heart free from sin and death to embrace his gift of new life.

Tonight, in faith and hope, let us renew our baptismal promises to the Risen Lord in whom death is no more. Let us celebrate in joy his spirit of love among us, transforming all humanity – indeed creation itself.

Rev. Michael Traher, SFM

People and Prayers to Remember Today

Readings of the Day

Genesis 1.1 – 2.2
Psalm 104 or Psalm 33
Genesis 22.1-18
Psalm 16
Exodus 14.15-31; 15.20, 1 (Canada)
Exodus 14.15 – 15.1 (USA)
Exodus 15
Isaiah 54.5-14
Psalm 30

Isaiah 55.1-11
Isaiah 12
Baruch 3.9-15, 32 – 4.4
Psalm 19
Ezekiel 36.16-17a, 18-28
Psalm 42 or Psalm 51
Romans 6.3-11
Psalm 118
Matthew 28.1-10

Responding to the Word

Paul reminds us that through our baptism we have been deeply united to the mystery of Christ's death and resurrection. What can I do to be better united to Christ today?

Final Thoughts ...

Easter Sunday

CHRISTIAN CHURCHES AROUND the world proclaim the greatest good news ever told in human history: Christ has risen from the dead! What makes our joy still greater is that, as St. Paul puts it, we are "raised with Christ." His resurrection opens up forever the future of humankind and of creation. Both our present and our future shine from the radiant light of Christ's victory over death.

Such radiant light first illuminated the women who went to Jesus' tomb after the Sabbath and saw that the stone had been rolled away. At that very tomb, Mary Magdalene had an encounter with the Risen Lord. On the same day, the apostles were blessed when Jesus appeared to them, comforting them with the gift of peace and commissioning them to proclaim to the world the good news of his resurrection.

As we celebrate this Eucharist, the Risen Lord is in our midst, and the paschal candle lit on this very day stands as a reminder of how the resurrection of Christ enlightens every moment and every aspect of our lives. Like Mary Magdalene and the apostles, we, too, are commissioned to share the light, the peace and the joy that the resurrection of Christ has brought to our own lives. Let us sing – and bring other people to sing along with us – heartfelt and heart-filling alleluias.

Jean-Pierre Prévost

People and Prayers to Remember Today

Readings of the Day

Acts 10.34a, 37-43
Psalm 118
Colossians 3.1-4
or 1 Corinthians 5.6b-8

John 20.1-18
or Matthew 28.1-10
or Luke 24.13-35

Responding to the Word

Paul knows that we will be changed by our experience of Christ. How has my experience of Christ changed me during this past Lent?

Final Thoughts ...

2nd Sunday of Easter

TODAY'S GOSPEL MIGHT make us feel unsettled – and not only because, like Thomas, we sometimes struggle with doubt in our relationship with God. We may also feel uncomfortable with the invitation Jesus extends to us via Thomas, to touch the wounds of one another and to bring healing to those wounds.

Thomas' reaction to the news of the resurrection is born out of his feelings of grief, fear, hurt and anger. He challenges Jesus, throwing down the gauntlet with a threat that, without seeing and touching the wounds, he will not believe. Jesus accepts the challenge, guiding Thomas to feel the wounds of the crucifixion. Thomas is overcome with joy.

John vividly portrays Jesus' wounds as large and gaping. Thomas' hand can fit into Jesus' side; his finger can fit into the wounds on Jesus' hands. The fleshiness of this image is a gentle but insistent challenge to become bearers of Christ's peace. John invites us to respond to Jesus, who is calling us out of our hurts and fears to what the second reading calls "a new birth into a living hope."

Today, let us celebrate the hope that resolves doubt and heals wounds. Let us celebrate with the same joy that made Thomas proclaim, "My Lord and my God!" Let us be, like the first disciples, a living hope to the world.

Louise McEwan

People and Prayers to Remember this Week

Readings of the Day

Acts 2.42-47   1 Peter 1.3-9
Psalm 118   John 20.19-31

Responding to the Word

Thomas changes his doubts to firm faith when Jesus comes to him. How has my faith grown through this Lent and Easter season?

_____

_____

_____

_____

_____

_____

_____

_____

_____

_____

_____

_____

Final Thoughts ...

_____

_____

_____

_____

Feasts this Week

April 21	**St Anselm**
April 23	**St George**
	St Adalbert
April 24	**St Fidelis of Sigmaringen**
April 25	**St Mark**

3rd Sunday of Easter

HOW OFTEN HAVE we heard the expression "hindsight is 20/20." In the immediacy of the moment, our vision can be impaired by a lack of information. Today's Gospel presents such a situation.

Two disciples meet a stranger on their way to Emmaus and begin updating him on recent events: a prophet, a crucifixion, a missing body, angels. The stranger rebuffs them for their lack of vision and monopolizes the rest of the 7-mile walk with a treatise beginning with Moses and ending with Jesus, complete with scriptural references and two thousand years of prophecy.

Being disciples, they are hospitable and on their arrival in Emmaus, they encourage the stranger to stay the night. He takes them up on their offer, and blesses and breaks bread with them – a pivotal event through which the two disciples will re-interpret their walk with the stranger.

For he is no longer a stranger. He is Jesus! A walk that might have been tedious now becomes heart-burning and miraculous. What was perplexing is now understood.

The two can hardly wait to tell the others. Their tongues rejoice and in today's liturgy we're still hearing the echoes.

Their hindsight gives us insight into the ordinary events of our lives, into the presence of the Lord in the strangers with whom we walk. Today, may our hearts burn within us!

John Weir

People and Prayers to Remember this Week

Readings of the Day

Acts 2.14, 22-33   1 Peter 1.17-21
Psalm 16   Luke 24.13-35

Responding to the Word

Peter speaks to witness to what God has done for us through Jesus. What can I do today to give this same kind of witness?

Final Thoughts …

Feasts this Week

April 28	**St Peter Chanel**
	St Louis Grignion de Montfort
April 29	**St Catherine of Siena**
April 30	**St Marie of the Incarnation (Canada)**
	St Pius V (USA)
May 1	**St Joseph the Worker**
	St Pius V (Canada)
May 2	**St Athanasius**

4th Sunday of Easter

IN PASTORAL CARE, we often refer to "companions on the journey." These are the people who travel with us, particularly through the difficult times when we rely on another person for strength, guidance and comfort. In Christian life, we model our role of companion for others after Jesus Christ.

In today's readings, Jesus is presented as a shepherd. We know the shepherd as the one who stands between his sheep and all harm. Likewise, we know Jesus as the One who lays down his life for each of us. We know the shepherd as the one who leads the way. Likewise, we know Jesus as our guide who directs us on the right path, protecting us with his Spirit. We know the shepherd as the one whose voice his sheep recognize. Likewise, we know Jesus as the one who calls us each by name.

When many voices call out and many paths present themselves, and we truly need a companion on the journey, where do we encounter our shepherd? We encounter him in the remembrance and celebration of Jesus' sacrifice for us. But this is only the beginning. The companion we meet here journeys with us each day, protecting, guiding and calling us forth by name that we might have life and have it to the full.

Shelley Kuiack

People and Prayers to Remember this Week

Readings of the Day

Acts 2.14a, 36b-41   1 Peter 2.20b-25
Psalm 23   John 10.1-10

Responding to the Word

Personal conversion and baptism into the community are expected of new followers. What changes in my life do I seek during this Easter season?

Final Thoughts …

Feasts this Week

May 4	**Bl Marie-Léonie Paradis (Canada)**
May 6	**St François de Laval (Canada)**
May 8	**Bl Catherine of St Augustine (Canada)**

5th Sunday of Easter

TAKE A DEEP breath before you read today's Gospel. What you are about to read leaves reality TV shows in the dust. Telling his disciples that he will soon be leaving them and going to be with the Father, Jesus says, "The one who believes in me will also do the works that I do and, in fact, will do greater works than these."

We who are followers of Jesus are called not only to believe in him and to speak the good news of salvation to others: we are also expected to do what Jesus did. We all know what that looks like, and the list is quite long: heal the sick, comfort those in pain, protect the weak and vulnerable, embrace the poor, eat with sinners, defend the rights of those who are victimized, denounce injustice, and more. The task becomes more daunting when we realize that we ourselves are sinners. We may believe, but without the power and endless love that form the essence of the Son of God, how is it possible to do greater works than Jesus did?

People in Africa have a saying: The path is made by walking. Each time we show our faith by doing the things that Jesus did, we take another step toward being better believers than we were before. A challenge, yes. Possible? Without a doubt!

Susan Eaton

People and Prayers to Remember this Week

Readings of the Day —————————————————————

Acts 6.1-7   1 Peter 2.4-9
Psalm 33   John 14.1-12

Responding to the Word

The Twelve call others to service in the community. What new service can I offer to my community?

Final Thoughts …

Feasts this Week

May 12	**St Nereus and St Achilleus**
	St Pancras
May 13	**Our Lady of Fatima**
May 14	**St Matthias**
May 15	**St Isidore (USA)**

6th Sunday of Easter

IN THESE WEEKS after Easter we make our way through the Acts of the Apostles. We should really say the acts of the Holy Spirit, continuing the work of Christ and enabling his disciples to become like Christ. We see them preaching and working miracles like Christ. In today's reading we see them being persecuted by the same people who crucified Christ and, just as the cross gives the gospel its power, so the persecution of the apostles spreads the good news around the world.

In Samaria, Peter and John bestow the Spirit upon those who have been baptized into Christ. They have the power to do this because Christ has already bestowed the Spirit on them. John's Gospel repeatedly emphasizes that Christ's first and greatest gift is the gift of the Spirit, the Paraclete, who acts as our advocate and speaks through and for us: the Spirit of truth who leads believers into all truth. The Spirit dwells within our hearts, for the Spirit is love who unites us with the Father in Christ.

We should not think of the Spirit as a replacement for Christ, but rather as God uniting us with the Christ who lives in glory in the union of the Father. It is the glorification of this Christ that we celebrate in this Eucharist by the power of the Spirit.

Jennifer Cooper

People and Prayers to Remember this Week

Readings of the Day

Acts 8.5-8, 14-17

Psalm 66

1 Peter 3.15-18

John 14.15-21

Responding to the Word

Peter encourages us to be ready to share the reason for our hope. With whom might I share my hope today?

Final Thoughts …

Feasts this Week

May 18	**St John I**
May 20	**St Bernardine of Siena**
May 21	**St Eugène de Mazenod (Canada)**
	St Christopher Magallanes & Companions
	Ascension of the Lord (in some regions of the USA)
May 22	**St Rita of Cascia**

*Ascension of the Lord**

HE LIVED AMONG us. He died for us. He rose again to bring us new life. Now 40 days after Easter, we remember Jesus ascending into glory. For nearly two thousand years Christians have followed Jesus' command to "make disciples of all nations." The story of Jesus has been told in nearly all, if not all, of the over six thousand languages now spoken on earth.

Over 150 years ago, the first Christian missionaries made the arduous trek into the interior of the Yukon in Canada. They learned the languages of the Tutchone, G'witchin, Kaska and others. They shared with these northern peoples, in their own tongues, the truths Jesus had given.

Soon, over 90 per cent of the world's languages could be silenced due to the impact of globalization. Songs of praise to God will no longer be sung in many millennia-old languages.

Yet the story must continue to be told. "Why do you stand looking up toward heaven?" the angel chided, instructing the disciples to go out and tell the world about Jesus. We have the same message of the kingdom of God to bring to new generations. This story can best be told by our example: living as Jesus commanded us to live, for each other.

Michael Dougherty

* The 7th Sunday of Easter is celebrated in some diocese of the USA today. Refer to p. 105.

People and Prayers to Remember this Week

Readings of the Day

Acts 1.1-11
Psalm 47

Ephesians 1.17-23
Matthew 28.16-20

Responding to the Word

When Jesus ascends, he promises the Holy Spirit to help us continue his work of bringing others to him. What can I do to help someone learn about Christ today?

_____

_____

_____

_____

_____

_____

_____

_____

_____

_____

_____

_____

_____

Final Thoughts …

_____

_____

_____

_____

Feasts this Week

May 25	St Bede the Venerable
	St Gregory VII
	St Mary Magdalene de'Pazzi
May 26	St Philip Neri
May 27	St Augustine of Canterbury

7th Sunday of Easter (USA)

THE THEME OF today's readings takes us to a time and a place in the future. They take us beyond the immediate challenges that we are facing in our life and encourage us to trust in faith.

The psalm speaks of the orphans, the widows, the prisoners, the homeless. Each one is given what they need: a father for the orphans, a protector for the widow, prosperity to the prisoner, a home for the homeless.

While the struggles we live and the problems we face can often paralyze us in life and prevent us from living fully, today's readings open up a new horizon of possibilities. They stretch what is now and allow us to imagine what can be. We need not be stuck in our current state of struggle. We can overcome. But we need to trust in the profound goodness of God and his ability to transform our life. For him anything is possible.

The season of Easter attests to the biggest miracle of all – God raising his Son from death to life. God's ability to overturn situations of death and bring out new life when all seems lost is what shapes and increases our faith. Nothing is impossible for God. We have to remember and live according to this belief if we wish to see miracles in our lives.

Natalia Kononenko

People and Prayers to Remember this Week

Readings of the Day

Acts 1.12-14   1 Peter 4.13-16
Psalm 27   John 17.1-11a

Responding to the Word

The theme of suffering and deliverance is prevalent in today's readings. What suffering in my life am I seeking God to deliver me from most?

_____

_____

_____

_____

_____

_____

_____

_____

_____

_____

_____

_____

_____

_____

_____

_____

Final Thoughts ...

_____

_____

_____

_____

Feasts this Week

Refer to Feasts listed for May 24 Ascension of the Lord (p. 104).

Pentecost Sunday

IF YOU HAD a voice only your mother could love, could you sing a leading role in an opera? If you couldn't run faster than a snail, could you be a member of an Olympic track team?

There are times when we are asked to do something for which we feel entirely unqualified. Last Sunday, on the Ascension, the disciples were challenged to take the good news to the whole world. Lest such a task seem beyond their power, Jesus told them to wait until the Spirit came. They waited. The Spirit came. We celebrate that coming today, the feast of Pentecost.

The first reading tells us how the Holy Spirit descended upon Jesus' followers, giving them the power to reach out with the good news to all the nations of the world.

In the second reading, Paul tells us the Spirit enables us to say "Jesus is Lord." Then the gifts of the Holy Spirit inspire Christians to accomplish God's purpose for the world.

In the Gospel, John adds another dimension to what the Spirit gives us. We all are to forgive and heal one another. Too often we forget we have this power.

Though we are given the great challenge to bring all peoples to Christ, we cannot do this by ourselves. We can do it only in and through the Spirit.

Rev. John Spicer, CSsR

People and Prayers to Remember this Week

Readings of the Day

Acts 2.1-11

Psalm 104

1 Corinthians 12.3b-7, 12-13

John 20.19-23

Responding to the Word

The disciples are changed by their contact with the Holy Spirit. What changes has God brought about in me during this Easter season?

Final Thoughts ...

Feasts this Week

June 1	**Blessed Virgin Mary, Mother of the Church**
June 2	**St Marcellinus and St Peter**
June 3	**St Charles Lwanga & Companions**
June 5	**St Boniface**
June 6	**St Norbert**

Trinity Sunday

UNLIKE POPULAR UNDERSTANDING, today's celebration is not about dogmatic statements we cannot comprehend, but rather a love-party to which we are all invited. Scripture and tradition tell us that Father-Son-Spirit live in a perfect community of love. God, through Jesus in the Holy Spirit, has drawn all creation into that unceasing love, and continues to do so until the end of time.

This *mysterion* (Greek) of the Trinity invites us into an encounter, an experience of what it is like to be taken into a never-ending circle of love with a God who is "merciful and gracious, slow to anger, and abounding in steadfast love and faithfulness," who sent his Son not to condemn but to save, and who makes our hearts the dwelling place of the Holy Spirit.

After years of pain and suffering, my friend Jason's dim memory of God's perfect love was re-activated: "I met someone who loved me. It was most unusual, and I cried as soon as love touched me. I ran from it so many times because I was not used to love. A crust of ice had trapped my soul for many years. When love started to melt the ice, it hurt like thawing a frozen limb. It was torture, but slowly I began to feel alive in the pain. I returned time and again, until every inch of the frozen crust had melted. When I moved away, I didn't have to say goodbye. I took the place and the person with me. They had entered my heart." This is Trinity in action.

Marie-Louise Ternier-Gommers

People and Prayers to Remember this Week

Readings of the Day

Exodus 34.4b-6, 8-9

Daniel 3

2 Corinthians 13.11-13

John 3.16-18

Responding to the Word

Moses learns that God is merciful and gracious. Who or what has taught me most about God's mercy?

Final Thoughts ...

Feasts this Week

June 9	St Ephrem
June 11	St Barnabas
June 13	St Anthony of Padua

Body and Blood of Christ

CHRIST'S BODY CONTINUES to be broken and his blood shed today; we have yet to accept and cooperate with the presence and activity of Jesus in the world. In our Church, our world and our earth, Christ is suffering: in broken relationships and exclusion; among people at war and cities destroyed; in our polluted waters and soil; in inequitable access to resources. A message of hope is needed, a new way of living in the face of overwhelming need.

Christ gave us his body and blood, and continues to do so in every Eucharist, that we might be formed into his very self. He offers himself as food for our growth, food that prepares us for struggle and for loving, food that forms us as one body to live in solidarity, sharing so that each one has what is needed for life.

Christ's body is given and his blood outpoured when we give of ourselves. Wherever and whenever we offer a kind word or gesture; provide support for struggling people; give aid for the poor, hungry and homeless; advocate for justice: here, too, Christ is made present for others – healing, loving and sharing.

To eat of his body is to give ourselves for others and to live in Christ. In this we will have eternal life.

Sr. Carmen Diston, IBVM

People and Prayers to Remember this Week

Readings of the Day ——————————————

Deuteronomy 8.2-3, 14-16   1 Corinthians 10.16-17
Psalm 147   John 6.51-59

Responding to the Word

Sharing in the Eucharist brings us into greater communion, both with God and with others. What can I do to show this unity?

Final Thoughts …

Feasts this Week

June 19 **Most Sacred Heart of Jesus**
June 20 **Immaculate Heart of Mary**

12th Sunday in Ordinary Time

"BUT EVERYONE ELSE is doing it!" School kids teasing the loner? Executives padding their expense accounts? Neighbors gossiping about the family down the street? "Everyone else is doing it!" It's easy to just go with the flow, to abdicate responsibility for our own actions.

Deep down inside, we all realize that it doesn't matter what everyone else is doing – what matters is what we are doing. As followers of Jesus, we are called to witness to the truth of God's kingdom, regardless of what everyone else does. By doing what is right and just, we acknowledge God who is Lord of all life.

Easy to say, but much more difficult to live out in daily life.

Just ask the teenager who defies the bully at school. Or the person who stands up for what is right and risks ridicule, rejection or worse. Of all people, Jesus knew what can happen when we try to swim against the tide of popular opinion.

In today's Gospel, Jesus promises us that we will never be left alone when we try to do what is right. He doesn't say it will be easy. What he does say is that whenever we speak up for truth and justice, God is on our side, sustaining us and holding us up in difficult and challenging times. Indeed the Lord is with us!

Teresa Whalen Lux

People and Prayers to Remember this Week

Readings of the Day —————————————————

Jeremiah 20.10-13   Romans 5.12-15

Psalm 69   Matthew 10.26-33

Responding to the Word

Jesus' death and resurrection began the overthrow of evil's power in our world. What can I do today to increase the amount of good and lessen the amount of evil?

_____

_____

_____

_____

_____

_____

_____

_____

_____

_____

_____

Final Thoughts ...

_____

_____

_____

_____

Feasts this Week

June 22	St Paulinus of Nola
	St John Fisher and St Thomas More
June 24	Nativity of St John the Baptist
June 27	Bl Nykyta Budka and Bl Vasyl Velychkowsky (Canada)
	St Cyril of Alexandria

13th Sunday in Ordinary Time

WHEN I WAS an undergrad, I was told to read the Gospel of Matthew backwards, starting with the ending, the "Great Commission." Jesus' final words to his followers – "Go and make disciples of all nations" – resound in me and find a home in my heart, in the midst of the ordinariness of the end of school and the beginning of summer.

Today's Gospel occurs after Jesus calls each of his disciples by name, these very ordinary people who had commonplace lives marked by birth, growing up, marriage, children, work and death, much like our own hidden lives. Jesus calls these people out of their everyday existence to a spectacular purpose: working with him to bring about the kingdom of justice, peace and love in this world and to prepare for the next.

In calling them, in calling us through the baptism that Paul refers to, Jesus affords each of us a dignity, a purpose and a value unique to our gifts and capacities.

For some of us, we may be called to welcome the stranger, as the Shunammite woman did, to listen with patience and openness to the prophets in our midst, no matter how unwelcome their message might be. Or maybe we are simply called to respond to someone's need for a cold cup of water to offset the heat of a blazing summer sun.

Maureen Wicken

People and Prayers to Remember this Week

Readings of the Day

2 Kings 4.8-12a, 14-16
Psalm 89

Romans 6.3-4, 8-11
Matthew 10.37-42

Responding to the Word

Paul explains that those who have been baptized ought to die to sin and live faithfully. Which area of my life do I need to die to?

Final Thoughts ...

Feasts this Week

June 29	**St Peter and St Paul**
June 30	**First Martyrs of the Holy Roman Church**
July 1	**Canada Day (Canada)**
	St Junípero Serra (USA)
July 3	**St Thomas**
July 4	**St Elizabeth of Portugal (Canada)**
	Independence Day (USA)

14th Sunday in Ordinary Time

I AM WEARY. The yoke of responsibility rests heavily on my shoulders. Fretting, I glance down and see Sebastian lying at my feet. His uniquely speckled muzzle rests serenely on outstretched paws. He sleeps while I toil. At first I am jealous and then I remember.

Sebastian didn't always know how to rest. He came to me a wounded dog with a tattered past. His eyes were vacant and his body trembled. I felt overwhelmed and unequal to the training task at hand until a wise dog trainer came to save the day (and the dog). In the end, she needed to train me, not Sebastian! Slowly I learned to be "top dog." Gradually Sebastian recognized me as such and gladly relinquished his misguided attempts to guard the entire world against imminent disaster.

Sebastian sleeps at my feet while I sit and fret. Who is wise? Indeed mere infants (and even dogs!) know more than I. I too must relinquish control to my "alpha." Once I have done this I can stop guarding my food and anxiously watching shadows in the night. "Come to me, all you that are weary... and I will give you rest." Now I understand. For the most part I live my life as if I am God. No wonder I am weary. Sebastian, what a good dog. You teach your mistress well!

Karen Johnson

People and Prayers to Remember this Week

Readings of the Day

Zechariah 9.9-10   Romans 8.9, 11-13
Psalm 145   Matthew 11.25-30

Responding to the Word

The messianic king is a gentle ruler who brings peace. When have you experienced the peace of Jesus?

Final Thoughts ...

Feasts this Week

July 6	**St Maria Goretti**
July 9	**St Augustine Zhao Rong & Companions**
July 11	**St Benedict**

15th Sunday in Ordinary Time

WORDS, WORDS, WORDS. They persuade us to buy lots of stuff. They give us more information than at any time in human history. They wound hearts and launch wars. They cement relationships, make promises, console those who are suffering and bring hope to those in despair. Words make things happen.

Into this world of words comes God's word from a different time and culture, often using unfamiliar images. It seems so fragile. Can a story of a sower broadcasting seeds along the roadside compete with music videos and text messaging? with marketers' words backed by six-figure budgets? with 24/7 talk radio?

Faith says yes. Faith remembers that this word brought creation to life: "Let there be light...."

It remembers "I will be your God, you will be my people." It remembers "Go and sin no more." It remembers "Go, make disciples." It remembers the Word-made-flesh. The remembering isn't just for the past, however. As with all biblical remembering, God's word acts now, itself embedded in our history, creating, covenanting, forgiving, empowering. That's why proclaiming the Scriptures at liturgy is more than reading – it's an event in which God acts.

This Living Verb, Jesus Christ, Word-made-flesh speaks to hearts, minds, imaginations, hopes and desires. The message? Life – a hundredfold. Not a new communication technology, but a new relationship. Learn to listen; dare to respond – it's worth your life.

Bernadette Gasslein

People and Prayers to Remember this Week

Readings of the Day

Isaiah 55.10-11

Psalm 65

Romans 8.18-23

Matthew 13.1-23

Responding to the Word

Paul tells us that we, along with all creation, are in the process of being transformed by God's grace. What transformation would I most like God to bring about?

Final Thoughts ...

Feasts this Week

July 13	**St Henry**
July 14	**St Camillus de Lellis (Canada)**
	St Kateri Tekakwitha (USA)
July 15	**St. Bonaventure**
July 16	**Our Lady of Mount Carmel**
July 18	**St Camillus de Lellis (USA)**

16th Sunday in Ordinary Time

NATURE PROVIDES MANY metaphors for the kingdom of God. For instance, a garden or a farm usually has desirable plants plus weeds. Similarly, faith communities are made up of imperfect individuals at various stages of spiritual growth. In the first parable in today's Gospel, the farmer does not weed his field because that might also damage the good plants. So too God does not "prune" the community of believers, but waits until each person's true nature is revealed. Like the farmer, God is patient, allowing us time to mature, recognizing that something that initially looks undesirable might turn out to be something very good.

The parables of the mustard seed and the leaven show that something quite small can have a very large effect. The tiniest seed grows into a large tree, while a small bit of yeast leavens an entire batch of flour. Thus, those who think God is only in magnificent buildings, major events or important people may be blind to God's activity in and through what appears to be less significant. But some of the greatest saints had humble beginnings and spent their lives doing "little" things. We need to be open to the next Francis of Assisi, Thérèse of Lisieux or Mother Teresa. The kingdom of heaven really is like a mustard seed or a pinch of yeast.

John L. McLaughlin

People and Prayers to Remember this Week

_____

_____

_____

Readings of the Day ─────────────────────

Wisdom 12.13, 16-19   Romans 8.26-27
Psalm 86   Matthew 13.24-43

Responding to the Word

Jesus tells us that God's presence (kingdom) often starts out very small but can grow very large. How has my awareness of God grown recently?

_____

_____

_____

_____

_____

_____

_____

_____

_____

_____

Final Thoughts ...

Feasts this Week

July 20	**St Apollinaris**
July 21	**St Lawrence of Brindisi**
July 22	**St Mary Magdalene**
July 23	**St Bridget**
July 24	**St Sharbel Makhlūf**
July 25	**St James**

17th Sunday in Ordinary Time

THE GOSPEL TODAY is rich in images: buried treasure, fine pearls, nets full of fish. But then it ends on a frightening note of "weeping and gnashing of teeth" for the wicked. With a sigh of relief we remember that the net collects all manner of fish, regardless of quality. It even includes the clam which, though ugly in appearance, is the source of the "fine pearl."

Unlike other precious stones, the pearl originates in a living thing, a speck of foreign matter that has found its way into the embryo. Instead of the stranger being rejected, it is wrapped by the mother in "swaddling clothes," nurtured and, in the end, becomes precious beyond wildest dreams.

With Solomon today we pray for "a wise and discerning mind," one that recognizes the potential for goodness in everyone, regardless of our own prejudices or discomfort. We pray for wisdom that opens us to even a speck of goodness, both in the friend and in the stranger. We pray for faith to believe that grace will embrace and nourish that goodness as something precious to the Lord.

In Paul's words, we are all called and justified – the strong and the weak, the friend and the stranger – for we are on a journey that by grace will end not in punishment but in glory.

Br. Fred Sherrer, FSC

People and Prayers to Remember this Week

Readings of the Day

1 Kings 3.5-12
Psalm 119

Romans 8.28-30
Matthew 13.44-52

Responding to the Word

Jesus tells us that to gain God's kingdom we have to sacrifice what we now have. What must I give up to have God more fully in my life?

Final Thoughts ...

Feasts this Week

July 29	**St Martha**
July 30	**St Peter Chrysologus**
July 31	**St Ignatius of Loyola**
August 1	**St Alphonsus Liguori**

18th Sunday in Ordinary Time

"WE'RE HAVING A loaves-and-fishes meal tonight!" That's a saying that my family often hears me use when supplies are running low. On such occasions I attempt to create dinner out of whatever I have at hand, with varying degrees of success.

Today's familiar Gospel describes a scene of overflowing abundance, not just of food but, more significantly, of Jesus' own self. Jesus has just learned of the grisly death of his cousin, John the Baptist. Worn out by grief as well as the constant demands of his ministry, he seeks some time alone. No sooner does he go ashore, however, than he is met by a crowd clamoring for his attention. Moved by compassion, he puts aside his own needs in order to minister to them.

When the issue of food arises, it is worth noting that Jesus first tells the disciples themselves to feed the people. Every time we break and share bread in the Eucharist we hear the words, "Do this in memory of me." The challenge Jesus puts before us is the call to share with others, not only our bread but our very selves.

Whenever this seems impossible, when we feel inadequate, when we have little compassion or energy left, it is good to remember the loaves and fishes: like us, humble offerings that in the hands of Jesus can become a miracle.

Krystyna Higgins

People and Prayers to Remember this Week

_____

_____

_____

Readings of the Day ——————————————

Isaiah 55.1-3   Romans 8.35, 37-39
Psalm 145   Matthew 14.13-21

Responding to the Word

Paul thinks that nothing can separate us from the love of God. What has felt like a barrier separating me from God's love?

_____

_____

_____

_____

_____

_____

_____

_____

_____

_____

_____

_____

_____

_____

_____

_____

_____

_____

Final Thoughts ...

_____

_____

_____

Feasts this Week

August 4	**St John Mary Vianney**
August 5	**Dedication of the Basilica of St Mary Major**
	Bl Frédéric Janssoone (Canada)
August 6	**Transfiguration of the Lord**
August 7	**St Sixtus II & Companions**
	St Cajetan
August 8	**St Dominic**

19th Sunday in Ordinary Time

WHAT IF PETER had listened the first time? "Take heart, it is I; do not be afraid," Jesus told him when Peter became fearful at seeing Christ walk on water. Why did Peter have to ask for proof? And why such dramatic proof?

How different might the story have been if Peter had calmed down, sat back and waited for Jesus to reach the boat. On the surface, not much would have changed. The wind would have ceased, and the disciples would still have that revelation of the reality of Jesus.

Most paintings of this scene show a stern, commanding Jesus on the water. However, by now, Jesus must have known what to expect from Peter. Perhaps a knowing, loving grin might be more appropriate for these portraits. That's how I like to imagine Christ when I finally realize the truth of a situation. Like Peter, I take a lot of convincing, especially when God is involved. We long for instant solutions and dramatic signs. We are all Peter.

If Peter had thought a moment, he might have taken a lesson from Elijah, who waited for the silence. We're not good at silence. And we're not good at listening, especially listening to God. Perhaps we all need to pray often the first verse of today's Psalm, "Let me hear what God the Lord will speak."

Margaret Bick

People and Prayers to Remember this Week

Readings of the Day

1 Kings 19.9, 11-13
Psalm 85

Romans 9.1-5
Matthew 14.22-33

Responding to the Word

Paul would do anything to help others come to Christ. What can I do today to draw someone closer to Christ?

Final Thoughts ...

Feasts this Week

August 10	**St Lawrence**
August 11	**St Clare**
August 12	**St Jane Frances de Chantal**
August 13	**St Pontian and St Hippolytus**
August 14	**St Maximilian Kolbe**
August 15	**Assumption of the Blessed Virgin Mary**

Assumption of the Blessed Virgin Mary

TODAY IN LUKE'S Gospel, Mary visits Elizabeth. The scene is an intimate one of feeling, knowing and seeing God beneath the surface of their encounter. Upon hearing Mary's greeting, Elizabeth feels the child in her womb leap for joy. She immediately sees Mary's blessedness. Elizabeth has the insight of faith. She is filled with the Holy Spirit and proclaims what the Spirit reveals to her.

This Scripture reading is both inspiration and challenge. Elizabeth, who understood her own blessing in conceiving a child in her advanced years, also recognizes and proclaims Mary's great faith and the power of the Holy Spirit at work in Mary. These two women's radical openness to the Holy Spirit is inspirational. They are both able to recognize as well as respond to God's presence in their midst.

Mary and Elizabeth's deep responses to the Holy Spirit also offer us a challenge. Are we open, as were Elizabeth and Mary, to recognize God's presence in our midst? Are we willing to respond with such faith and witness?

Let us give thanks for the inspiration and faith of Mary and Elizabeth. May we be open to the Holy Spirit in our lives so that we too may feel, see, know and respond to God's presence in our encounters with one another.

Beth McIsaac Bruce

People and Prayers to Remember this Week

Readings of the Day —————————

Revelation 11.19a; 12.1-6a, 10ab 1 Corinthians 15.20-27
Psalm 45   Luke 1.39-56

Responding to the Word

Elizabeth experienced God's wonderful power to work a miracle in her life. What miracles can I see in my life?

Final Thoughts ...

20th Sunday in Ordinary Time

TODAY'S GOSPEL ABOUT the woman from Canaan is a demonstration of God's kindness. It also highlights the virtues of faith, humility and perseverance. When Jesus did not heed her request the first time, and his disciples urged him to ignore her, the Canaanite woman fell to her knees and humbled herself before him. Moved by her faith, Jesus cured her daughter. There was something about her faith and humility and her unwillingness to get discouraged that impressed Jesus. She believed in him, and she came out of that encounter refreshed and renewed.

Jesus' mercy and justice shine through in this encounter. We can imitate his example and open our hearts to all people, no matter where they come from, no matter what the difficulties are. For it is only through this openness of spirit that we communicate and share with everyone the essence of God's love. Reverend Richard Humke, an Episcopalian priest, has noted: "In the context of the Lord's supper, where we all come knowing that none of us is perfect and that each of us has failed... something good happens in our life as a community when we notice the people around us." Jesus noticed the woman from Canaan for her faith. "Woman, great is your faith!"

Jesus invites us to open our hearts and believe.

Sharon Queano

People and Prayers to Remember this Week

Readings of the Day

Isaiah 56.1, 6-7   Romans 11.13-15, 29-32
Psalm 67   Matthew 15.21-28

Responding to the Word

The persistent woman will accept no excuse from Jesus about why he will not heal her daughter. For what am I continually asking Jesus in my prayer?

Final Thoughts ...

Feasts this Week

August 19	**St John Eudes**
August 20	**St Bernard**
August 21	**St Pius X**
August 22	**Queenship of the Blessed Virgin Mary**

21st Sunday in Ordinary Time

TODAY, BOTH JESUS and Simon Peter receive new names. In response to Jesus' question – "Who do you say that I am?" – Simon Peter identifies Jesus not only as Messiah but with a new title: Son of the living God.

Simon Peter's profound confession of faith is itself a gift of God. Peter did not come to this knowledge all on his own. The Father-Son language he uses emphasizes the unique relationship between Jesus and the one God. Peter's profession of faith also identifies the type of Messiah Jesus is: a suffering servant who lays down his life out of love, and achieves the salvation planned for us by the living God from the very beginning.

On the basis of such faith in Christ – and on this basis alone – Simon is now renamed Peter, the rock (in Greek *petra*) on whose faith the Church will be built. Not even God will contest his judgments because Christ will be at their very core.

We, too, have been renamed. Given the gift of faith and adopted as children of God in baptism, we Christians now share in Jesus' unique relationship with the Father. We say daily through word and deed who Jesus is. If our witness is lacking, and it often is, we need only renew our faith, reminding ourselves in gratitude of God's profound love for us.

Christine Mader

People and Prayers to Remember this Week

Readings of the Day

Isaiah 22.15, 19-23   Romans 11.33-36
Psalm 138   Matthew 16.13-20

Responding to the Word

Jesus demands that his disciples understand who he is. How would I answer Jesus' question today?

Final Thoughts ...

Feasts this Week

August 24	**St Bartholomew**
August 25	**St Louis**
	St Joseph Calasanz
August 27	**St Monica**
August 28	**St Augustine**
August 29	**Passion of St John the Baptist**

22nd Sunday in Ordinary Time

WE HUMAN BEINGS are symbol-makers. Since the dawn of time people give meaning to their lives through symbols and other forms of artistic expression. The cross of Jesus is an important symbol of meaning in our religious tradition. Mel Gibson's *Passion of the Christ* captured the imagination of many people, Christian and non-Christian alike. The question whether many who saw the movie have returned to their churches still remains unanswered. But we may ask: When do symbols lose their meaning?

In today's Gospel Jesus is clear about the meaning of the cross. The cross is a symbol of dying to all selfishness and exaggerated self-importance. The cross of Jesus is a constant reminder to us as persons and as communities of the need to adjust our attitudes and priorities regarding God and God in our neighbor. If anyone wants to follow Jesus on the Way, they must "deny [themselves] and take up [their] cross and follow" the Teacher. To step down from our pedestal of illusory greatness is the symbolic meaning of the cross.

We begin and end the Eucharist with the sign of the cross. As bread and wine are transformed into Jesus' body and blood, let this sign transform our minds and hearts so we may become authentic disciples of hope in a crucified world. "Go in the peace of Christ."

Rev. Robert F. Dueweke, OSA

People and Prayers to Remember this Week

Readings of the Day

Jeremiah 20.7-9   Romans 12.1-2
Psalm 63   Matthew 16.21-27

Responding to the Word

Paul encourages us to be transformed so we know what is good and pleasing to God. What do I most need to change in my life to be more pleasing to God?

Final Thoughts ...

Feasts this Week

September 2	**Bl André Grasset (Canada)**
September 3	**St Gregory the Great**
September 4	**Bl Dina Bélanger (Canada)**

23rd Sunday in Ordinary Time

IN TODAY'S FIRST reading, Ezekiel receives a command: warn Israel to turn away sharply from its current, perilous lifestyle. Underlying this stark warning is the intense passion of God for their well-being, and God's invitation to return again to safety through obedience to the voice of their shepherd.

How we hate to be reprimanded for wrongdoing: we feel embarrassed and humbled. In the Gospel today, Jesus teaches us how to help each other overcome the hurt caused by our sinfulness. Correction of a community member is to be done lovingly and with care. In this manner, the offender is helped to change and is restored to wholeness as a person; they can then live fully and freely in relationship to God and others.

What happens on a personal level can lead, on a larger scale, to the healing of communities and nations. Ezekiel's mission could equally be applied to our world today and the painful condition of whole nations – indeed, of creation itself. God's passion is for all peoples to live in peace, dignity and freedom, and for the gifts of creation to be respected and shared fairly. We are charged by Christ to do all that we can to restore life and promote healing among ourselves and for creation. As Christians we are, by vocation, healers and reconcilers to the world around us.

Rev. Michael Traher, SFM

People and Prayers to Remember this Week

Readings of the Day ────────────────

Ezekiel 33.7-9   Romans 13.8-10
Psalm 95   Matthew 18.15-20

Responding to the Word

**Paul declares that loving one another is what God requires.
What might I do to show my love for others today?**

Final Thoughts …

Feasts this Week

September 8	**Nativity of the Blessed Virgin Mary**
September 9	**St Peter Claver**
September 12	**Most Holy Name of Mary**

24th Sunday in Ordinary Time

THE WORLD WAS stunned in 1981 as television screens filled with reports of the attempted assassination of Pope John Paul II. Seriously wounded, the Pope recovered and later visited his assailant and forgave him. In that same decade the brutal system of apartheid was dismantled and Nelson Mandela was released from prison. Even though he had been unjustly imprisoned, he, along with other leaders, worked for reconciliation, not revenge against his oppressors.

These are dramatic responses to the mandate from today's Gospel. Peter asks, "How often should I forgive? As many as seven times?" Jesus gives a direct and certain answer: "Not seven times, but, I tell you, seventy-seven times." In other words, our response to injury or injustice must always be forgiveness. I suspect Peter had hoped for a different answer.

We see rejection of the gospel of forgiveness in a world grown accustomed to war, gun violence and domestic violence. To move toward forgiveness, even in these extreme situations, is to believe love is stronger than hate and that God can heal the human heart.

If we take seriously Jesus' command to forgive, we are challenged to see what divisions exist in our families, workplaces, neighborhoods. Naming them alone does not bring about forgiveness, but God working through a heart open to conversion does. The forgiven can become the forgiving.

Sr. Judy Morris, OP

People and Prayers to Remember this Week

Readings of the Day

Sirach 27.30 – 28.7
Psalm 103

Romans 14.7-9
Matthew 18.21-35

Responding to the Word

Jesus comes so we might have eternal life with God. When have I felt the stirrings of this new life with God?

Final Thoughts ...

Feasts this Week

September 14	**Exaltation of the Holy Cross**
September 15	**Our Lady of Sorrows**
September 16	**St Cornelius and St Cyprian**
September 17	**St Robert Bellarmine**
September 19	**St Januarius**

25th Sunday in Ordinary Time

TODAY'S GOSPEL, THE parable of the landowner and the laborers, begins with negotiation and recruiting, and ends with payday. I couldn't find a middle. What fruitful labor are the workers called to and paid for? What do they accomplish? It is as if the landowner calls the workers unconditionally, saying, "Come on in. I will pay you a just wage. You have nothing better to do, so let's see what happens under these conditions."

And what conditions they are! Negotiations begin. The usual daily wage is established. Flexible hours are encouraged. Idle workers are recruited. Grumbling is not allowed. The employer is generous.

What an opportunity! Perhaps there is no middle to this parable because these conditions rarely exist in the real world. Today 20 per cent of the world's population consumes more than 80 per cent of the earth's resources. One billion people go to bed hungry every night. Such an imbalance could not exist in the vineyard of today's Gospel.

We are invited to be like the landowner: flexible, fair, generous. We can "fill in the blanks" of this parable with justice for workers and an equitable distribution of God's earthly gifts.

John Weir

People and Prayers to Remember this Week

_____

_____

_____

Readings of the Day —————————————————

Isaiah 55.6-9   Philippians 1.20-24, 27
Psalm 145   Matthew 20.1-16

Responding to the Word

In Jesus' parable, the workers grumble about the landowner's generosity. How might I imitate God's generosity in my dealings with others today?

_____

_____

_____

_____

_____

_____

_____

_____

_____

_____

_____

_____

_____

_____

_____

_____

_____

_____

_____

_____

Final Thoughts ...

_____

_____

_____

_____

Feasts this Week

September 21	**St Matthew**
September 23	**St Pius of Pietrelcina**
September 24	**Bl Emilie Tavernier-Gamelin (Canada)**
September 25	**St Cosmas and St Damian (Canada)**
September 26	**St John de Brébeuf, St Isaac Jogues & Companions (Canada)**
	St Cosmas and St Damian (USA)

26th Sunday in Ordinary Time

I ONCE HAD the good fortune to meet a woman who, on the exterior, was materially poor. She appeared to me a simple person. Then she spoke. She told me how fortunate "we" are in this society. "We have so much. We have electricity and water and there are people in the Third World who don't even have anything to eat. We are so lucky for all that we have – and we take it for granted."

On that particular day, I was feeling sorry for myself. This woman challenged me to face my self-absorption and therefore my "no" to laboring in God's vineyard. Her keen ability to point to God's kingdom moved me to gratitude and solidarity.

When we consider the parable of the two sons in today's Gospel, we are invited to listen to those who labor in God's vineyard. We are challenged to become aware of the subtle ways that we can be distracted, self-absorbed and say no to God in our neighbors, when we should be listening to their witness as a means to turn away from our selfishness and toward our neighbors in need.

Let us give thanks to God for giving us laborers whose witness can transform us. May the Holy Spirit continue to help us to follow Christ by faithfully laboring in God's vineyard.

Beth McIsaac Bruce

People and Prayers to Remember this Week

Readings of the Day ———————————————

Ezekiel 18.25-28
Psalm 25

Philippians 2.1-11
Matthew 21.28-32

Responding to the Word

Jesus' parable describes the contrasting attitudes of two sons. Which of the two sons have I been like this week?

Final Thoughts …

Feasts this Week

September 28	**St Wenceslaus**
	St Lawrence Ruiz & Companions
September 29	**St Michael, St Gabriel and St Raphael**
September 30	**St Jerome**
October 1	**St Thérèse of the Child Jesus**
October 2	**Holy Guardian Angels**

27th Sunday in Ordinary Time

EVERYBODY KNOWS SOMEONE who thinks the world owes them a living. Psychologists call this having a sense of entitlement. A sense of entitlement dulls, or even kills, a person's ability to feel thankful. If I deserve everything I get (or want), there is no room for gratitude.

The plants in the vineyard, the tenants in Jesus' story and the authorities in Jerusalem seem to have suffered from a sense of entitlement. The ungrateful vines produced sour grapes. The tenants failed to recognize their interdependent partnership with the landlord. The Jerusalem authorities saw their social status as a sign of God's approval, a sign of their salvation. The problem is not that they failed to "earn their keep," it's that their sense of entitlement hobbled their ability to respond with gratitude to what they had received.

The weekly Sunday Eucharist trains us in this attitude. As the Greek name indicates (*eucharistia* = thanksgiving), thanksgiving is at the heart of our Sunday gathering. The eucharistic prayer is the Church's great prayer of thanks at the banquet table of the Lord. What prayers of thanksgiving do you bring along to Mass today? What fruits do your gifts call you to bring forth to the world?

Margaret Bick

People and Prayers to Remember this Week

Readings of the Day ————————————

Isaiah 5.1-7
Psalm 80

Philippians 4.6-9
Matthew 21.33-43

Responding to the Word

Paul urges us to let go of our anxieties and turn in prayer to God. What anxieties make it hard for me to pray right now?

Final Thoughts …

Feasts this Week

October 5	**Bl Francis Xavier Seelos (USA)**
October 6	**St Bruno**
	Bl Marie-Rose Durocher
October 7	**Our Lady of the Rosary**
October 9	**St Denis & Companions**
	St John Leonardi

28th Sunday in Ordinary Time

TODAY'S READINGS SPEAK of abundance: Isaiah of a feast, the psalmist of an overflowing cup, and Paul of a God who satisfies every need. Matthew tells the story of a lavish wedding banquet, of the many who refuse to attend, and then of the one who is mysteriously thrown outside. We search for understanding.

Jesus is a practical teacher: we can relate to his examples. If the kingdom of God is like a wedding feast, we can imagine invitations, good company and good food. We know the usual reply is an immediate and eager "yes." Yet this is a story both of ongoing refusal and of consistent determination that this kingdom feast will be filled.

As the celebration finally begins, we are speechless as one of the guests is cast out for improper attire. Perhaps he was not invited to be a mere guest. Perhaps he was invited to be the bride: a symbol of his deep, faithful and lasting relationship with the Son of the Father. Of course he would need a wedding robe: a special and beautiful garment made of such qualities as kindness, justice, humility, love and compassion.

We are all invited to share in the banquet and to wear the wedding robe. Simple? Yes. Easy? Not always. We are all called and chosen. Today, we accept the treasured invitation and celebrate this feast with joy.

Brenda Merk Hildebrand

People and Prayers to Remember this Week

Readings of the Day —————————————————

Isaiah 25.6-10a
Psalm 23

Philippians 4.12-14, 19-20
Matthew 22.1-14

Responding to the Word

Isaiah encourages us to rejoice and be glad for God has saved us. How can I thank God today for all God has done for me?

_____

_____

_____

_____

_____

_____

_____

_____

_____

Final Thoughts ...

_____

_____

_____

_____

Feasts this Week

October 12	**Thanksgiving Day (Canada)**
October 14	**St Callistus I**
October 15	**St Teresa of Jesus**
October 16	**St Marguerite d' Youville (Canada)**
	St Hedwig (USA)
	St Margaret Mary Alacoque (USA)
October 17	**St Ignatius of Antioch**

29th Sunday in Ordinary Time

WE ALL HAVE significant relationships: a school friend, a family member, a spouse, or a member of a community or movement. We desire to love and be loved, and to live a meaningful life. Relationships can be exciting, affirming and fulfilling; they might also be unsettling or even scary as we explore what a particular relationship offers.

Today's readings invite us to ponder God's relationship with us. As with Cyrus, God chose you and me, called us each by name. God is here before and beside us, surrounding us with the gifts and grace to do God's work.

In the readings of the last few Sundays, Jesus calls us to focus our minds, hearts and lives on him. We are urged to show respect, to use the gifts God has given us and to reach out to the poor without exclusion. In today's Gospel the chief priests and Pharisees are reluctant to examine themselves. As they try to entrap Jesus, they struggle with their loyalties and what a relationship with Jesus asks of them. These are often our struggles, too. Jesus invites us to be faithful in our loving and generous in our living. We are called to follow him wholeheartedly and without reservation.

Sr. Carmen Diston, IBVM

People and Prayers to Remember this Week

Readings of the Day

Isaiah 45.1, 4-6
Psalm 96

1 Thessalonians 1.1-5ab
Matthew 22.15-21

Responding to the Word

God governs political events even though political rulers do not know it. Where do I detect God's presence in political events today?

_____

_____

_____

_____

_____

_____

_____

_____

Final Thoughts ...

_____

_____

_____

_____

Feasts this Week

October 19	**St Paul of the Cross (Canada)**
	St John de Brébeuf, St Isaac Jogues & Companions (USA)
October 20	**St Hedwig (Canada)**
	St Margaret Mary Alacoque (Canada)
	St Paul of the Cross (USA)
October 22	**St John Paul II**
	Anniversary of Dedication of Churches whose date of consecration is unknown (Canada)
October 23	**St John of Capistrano**
October 24	**St Anthony Mary Claret**

30th Sunday in Ordinary Time

As THE END of the Church year nears, our readings contain warnings to be prepared to meet the Lord when he comes again. On the final Sunday of the year, Christ the King, we will hear how Christ will judge us: "just as you did it to one of the least... you did it to me."

Today's readings give us a heads-up, for their message is similar. The first reading says, "You shall not wrong or oppress... you shall not abuse any widow or orphan." In the Gospel, Jesus says there are two great commandments. To love God is the first; the second is similar: "You shall love your neighbor as yourself."

These two commandments sum up Scripture ("the Law and the Prophets"). God's message in a nutshell is to love God and love your neighbor. We show we love God by loving our neighbor. Faith is not just spiritual or intellectual. It demands our whole life; it must be lived.

We must be rooted, first, in our relationship with God. That relationship – our love for God – must bear fruit in love for others. Our relationship with God is made manifest – made credible – in our love for our neighbor.

And our neighbor is everyone, especially the weak, especially the needy. To revise the old maxim: "Neighborly-ness" is next to Godliness!

Dinah Simmons

People and Prayers to Remember this Week

Readings of the Day —————————————————

Exodus 22.20-26 (USA)
Exodus 22.21-27 (Canada)
Psalm 18

1 Thessalonians 1.5c-10
Matthew 22.34-40

Responding to the Word

Christianity is spread by good example more than words. Whose example has been most influential in making me a better Christian?

Final Thoughts ...

Feasts this Week

October 28   St Simon and St Jude

All Saints

THE FEAST OF All Saints is an occasion to remember and honor the women and men, known and unknown, who lived courageous lives with an unwavering faith in Jesus Christ.

I tend to regard the saints as a distinct group of individuals chosen by God: a people set apart. So when I read a statement by Mother Teresa that "to be a saint, you have to seriously want to be one," I was taken aback. I felt an invitation, even encouragement, to reflect on what I had chosen – in my life, with my life.

I have come to learn that these women and men struggled with their sinfulness, failures and life's disappointments. In their relationship with God, they were prone to doubts, confusion, selfishness and even anger. In other words, they were very much like us. Yet, despite their limitations and imperfections, they never gave up on saying "yes" to Christ. They continued to say "no" to worldly values and concerns. The saints, it seems, would not serve two masters.

They strove to be faithful to the kind of life the Beatitudes urge us to live – even to death. The saints' lives reveal that each of us is being called to live our life as a child of God, caring for peace, reconciliation and the poor. What will our response be to God's invitation?

Julie Cachia

People and Prayers to Remember this Week

Readings of the Day

Revelation 7.2-4, 9-14   1 John 3.1-3
Psalm 24   Matthew 5.1-12a

Responding to the Word

**In the Beatitudes, Jesus talks about ways of living that will
make one happy. Identify which Beatitude you need most in
your life.**

Final Thoughts ...

Feasts this Week

November 2	All Souls' Day
November 3	St Martin de Porres
November 4	St Charles Borromeo

32nd Sunday in Ordinary Time

"No fair!" Anyone who has spent time with young children is probably familiar with that cry of protest. Some of the parables in Scripture can, at first glance, provoke a similar reaction in us. Stories like the Prodigal Son, for example, or the workers in the vineyard who are all paid the same wage, can seem "unfair" to our limited human understanding. Today's Gospel is, I think, another such story.

Why are the five "wise" bridesmaids so unhelpful to their ill-prepared companions? Why is the bridegroom so inflexible, shutting the door without even acknowledging them? Is this "fair"?

Such stories are difficult for us to grasp with our limited human perceptions of justice. If God's love is comprehensive and unconditional, what are we to make of the unfortunate bridesmaids?

Yes, God's love is unconditional and all-embracing. However, that gift of love calls forth a response in us: the response of being ready and open to receive it. All of the bridesmaids fall asleep; but when they hear the call to meet the bridegroom, only the wise ones are prepared to answer that call.

The God of surprises beckons to us in the most unexpected circumstances. Let us pray that we may always keep the lamp of our heart lit so as to recognize and welcome the divine presence wherever it may be found.

Krystyna Higgins

People and Prayers to Remember this Week

Readings of the Day

Wisdom 6.12-16
Psalm 63

1 Thessalonians 4.13-18
Matthew 25.1-13

Responding to the Word

Wisdom is found by those who seek her. Where have I found wisdom in my life?

Final Thoughts ...

Feasts this Week

November 9	**Dedication of the Lateran Basilica**
November 10	**St Leo the Great**
November 11	**St Martin of Tours**
November 12	**St Josaphat**
November 13	**St Frances Xavier Cabrini (USA)**

33rd Sunday in Ordinary Time

WITHIN US IS a unique heart-song placed there by God. Our vocation is to sing the song and leave a voiceprint for others to hear. We might not be the first violin or the loudest trumpet, but without that one note from a simple triangle a symphony is incomplete.

We may think we are civilized, yet we are often confronted by evil wrought by human hands. This may be because we do not develop our talents and so make the world a better place. Have we became tone-deaf to God's heart-song? Have we buried our talent? If we risk nothing, we gain nothing. If we risk even a little and deposit just one talent, eternal reward can be ours.

Whenever time runs out, we typically muse about what might have been and regret what we have squandered or wasted. As this liturgical year draws to a close, let us not rue the past. Instead, let us rediscover our heart-song and help others discover theirs. Let us reach out with the power of that song and sing it loud and clear. Then, let us listen for the voice of the Master calling us home: "Well done." Our vocation is simply to receive from God the gift of who we are and return that gift to God through an authentic response.

Wanda Conway

People and Prayers to Remember this Week

Readings of the Day ——————————————

Proverbs 31.10-13, 19-20, 30-31
  (USA)
Proverbs 31.10-13, 16-18, 20,
  26, 28-31 (Canada)

Psalm 128
1 Thessalonians 5.1-6
Matthew 25.14-30

Responding to the Word

In Jesus' parable, the servants are accountable for the talents they are given. How am I using the talents that God has given me?

Final Thoughts ...

Feasts this Week

November 16	**St Margaret of Scotland**
	St Gertrude
November 17	**St Elizabeth of Hungary**
November 18	**Dedication of the Basilicas of Sts Peter and Paul**
	St Rose Philippine Duchesne (USA)
November 21	**Presentation of Blessed Virgin Mary**

Our Lord Jesus Christ, King of the Universe

ON THIS FEAST of Christ the King, the Gospel presents a secret that can revolutionize our lives and, indeed, our world: treat others as if they were Jesus. Of course, others may not look or behave or even smell like we imagine Jesus would, but that is not the point. We need to act as if this were true.

Jean Vanier, who founded L'Arche, had long lived with people who have intellectual disabilities. Instead of a society that is a pyramid – with a few wealthy, powerful people at the top and the poor crushed at the bottom, scrambling to get a little higher – Vanier invited us to image a society that is a circle, where everyone has a place. He often pointed out that when we make others feel they belong, we find that we also belong.

It's easy to miss the divine presence in others, even in those closest to us. One of the most courageous things we can do is to admit we have been blind, and then to change the way we act. As we live generously in our attitudes and actions toward others, we will discover God in every person – whether above or below, in front or behind – and we will be transformed into neighbors. We will have entered the realm of the blessed, where Jesus reigns.

Beth Porter

People and Prayers to Remember this Week

Readings of the Day

Ezekiel 34.11-12, 15-17   1 Corinthians 15.20-26, 28
Psalm 23   Matthew 25.31-46

Responding to the Word

**Our hope for new life means belonging fully to Christ now.
What can I do to offer myself completely to Christ?**

Final Thoughts ...

Feasts this Week

November 23   **St Clement I**
               St Columban
               Bl Miguel Agustín Pro (USA)
November 24   **St Andrew Dũng-Lạc & companions**
November 25   **St Catherine of Alexandria**
November 26   **Thanksgiving Day (USA)**

My Spiritual Journey